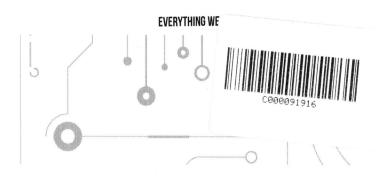

STAR WARS
THE FORCE AWAKENS:
EVERYTHING WE KNOW

BY THOM DADDLE

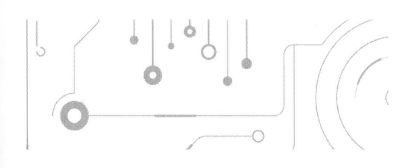

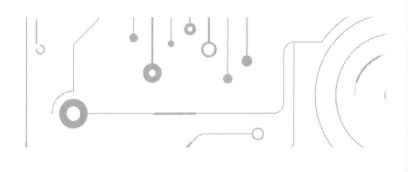

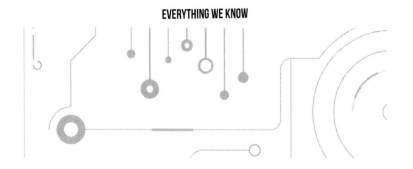

For the true believers...

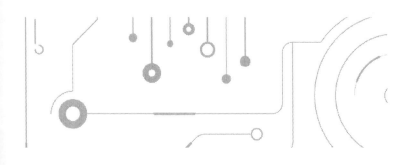

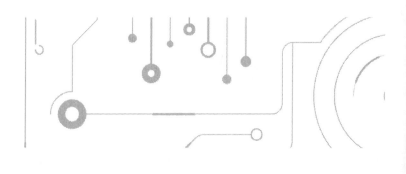

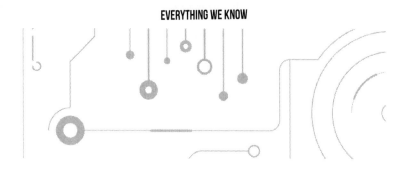

The Adventure Begins...

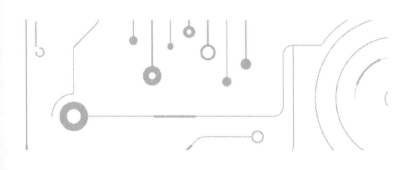

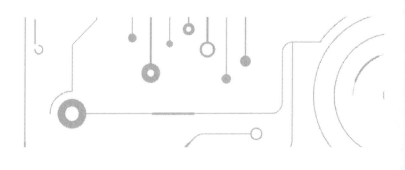

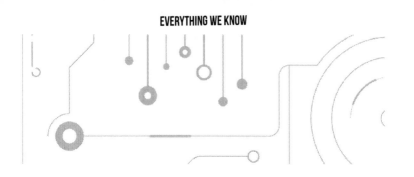

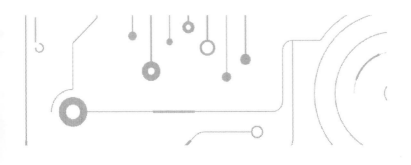

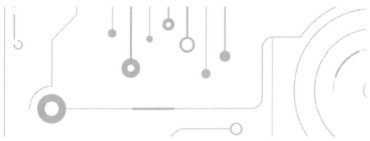

Star Wars: Episode VII The Force Awakens, marketed simply as *Star Wars: The Force Awakens,* is the upcoming seventh live-action theatrical *Star Wars* film and the first film of the sequel trilogy. The film is directed by J.J. Abrams, written by Abrams, Michael Arndt, and Lawrence Kasdan, and produced by Kathleen Kennedy and Bad Robot Productions. The film, which is currently in production, will be released on December 18, 2015. (December 17, in Mexico and the rest of Latin America)

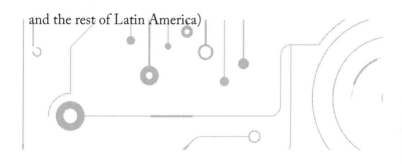

Despite initially claiming that the *Star Wars* story ended in *Star Wars: Episode VI Return of the Jedi*, and spending years refuting speculation that there would be another film, George Lucas began work on the story of *Episode VII* in 2011 in order to increase the value of Lucasfilm Ltd. before he sold it to The Walt Disney Company, although Disney would later elect not to use Lucas's story. The acquisition was finalized on October 30, 2012, and Disney and Lucasfilm officially announced Episode VII the same day.

The story of Episode VII is not yet known, but it will not be based on Star Wars Legends, formerly known as the Expanded Universe. Rather, it will be an original story set after Return of the Jedi. The film stars Mark Hamill, Harrison Ford, Carrie Fisher, Peter Mayhew, Anthony Daniels, and Kenny Baker reprising their original roles. The original actors are joined by a host of new actors including John Boyega, Daisy Ridley, and Adam Driver, amongst many others.

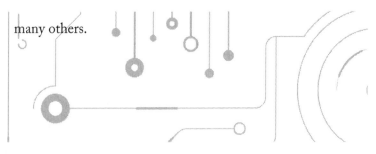

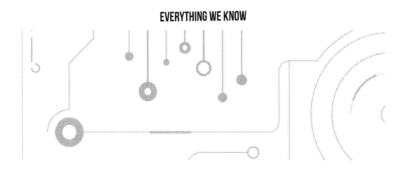

"I keep telling J.J. Abrams this is a $4 billion movie. We need to treat this very special. It's an unbelievable privilege and unbelievable responsibility to take a jewel and treat it in a way that is respectful of its past but brings it into the future."
- Bob Iger

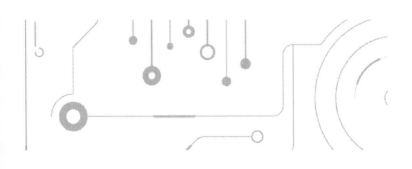

On October 30, 2012, The Walt Disney Company announced that it had purchased Lucasfilm Ltd., the production company behind the creation of the Star Wars franchise, from its owner, Star Wars creator George Lucas, for $4.05 billion. The acquisition came in the wake of Lucas's announced retirement on May 31, and the subsequent June 1 announcement that veteran film producer Kathleen Kennedy was succeeding Lucas as Lucasfilm's Co-Chair. As part of the merger, Disney revealed that it planned to

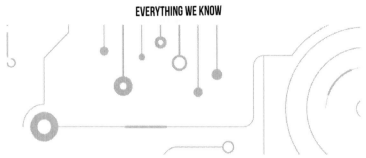

produce a sequel trilogy of films, beginning in 2015, that would include the long-awaited Episodes VII, VIII, and IX. Lucas will remain involved as a creative consultant, with Kennedy serving as executive producer.

Star Wars Episode VII had already been in development for several months as of the Disney–Lucasfilm merger. Lucas has written the story treatments for each of the three upcoming films. Kennedy said shortly after the

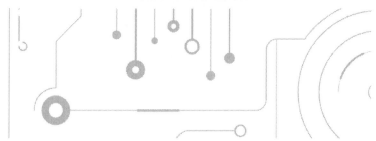

announcement that the development team was in the process of sitting down with writers to discuss story ideas. According to a Lucasfilm source, the basis for Star Wars Episode VII will be an original story, rather than taking inspiration from previous Expanded Universe content, such as author Timothy Zahn's The Thrawn Trilogy of novels, which chronologically follows the events of Star Wars: Episode VI Return of the Jedi in the Star Wars canon. This was later confirmed on April 25, 2014,

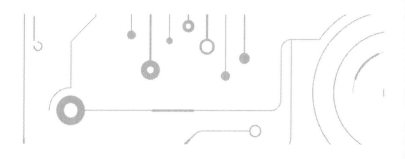

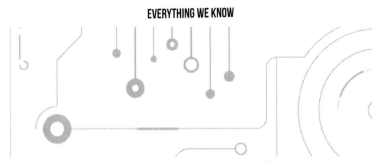

when Lucasfilm announced the creation of a new continuity

that includes the previous six episodic films, the Star Wars: The

Clone Wars TV series, and all future content beginning with the

forthcoming Star Wars Rebels TV series and the novel A New

Dawn.

Lucasfilm confirmed on November 9 that pre-production

had began on Star Wars Episode VII, and that screenwriter

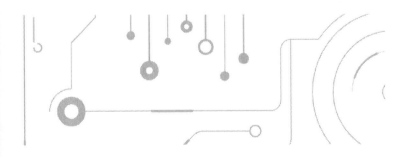

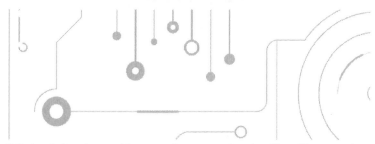

Michael Arndt would write the script for the film. News outlets

first reported Arndt's involvement on November 8, announcing

that, according to insiders, Arndt has already turned in a forty-

to-fifty-page story treatment that will reportedly bring the

Skywalker family saga to a close in a new trilogy. Reports first

announced on January 24, 2013 that J.J. Abrams, known for his

work on the television series Lost and the most recent entries

in the Star Trek film series, will direct Star Wars Episode VII

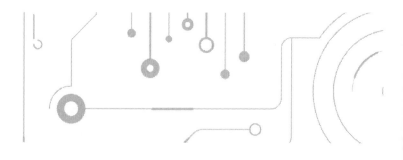

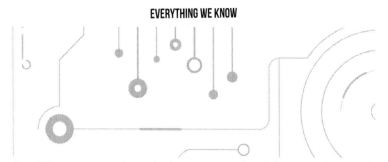

StarWars.com confirmed the reports the following day, with George Lucas remarking "I've consistently been impressed with J.J. as a filmmaker and storyteller. He's an ideal choice to direct the new Star Wars film and the legacy couldn't be in better hands."

According to reports, Lawrence Kasdan and Simon Kinberg would co-produce all three films of the upcoming sequel trilogy, and share writing responsibilities for both

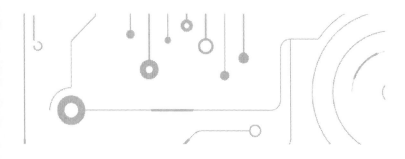

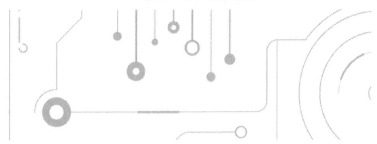

Star Wars Episodes VIII and IX. Kasdan originally wrote the screenplays for both Star Wars: Episode V The Empire Strikes Back and Star Wars Episode VI: Return of the Jedi. StarWars.com confirmed Kasdan's and Kinberg's involvement as project consultants for Star Wars Episode VII on January 25.

During a concert with the Young Musician's Foundation Debut Orchestra on February 9, John Williams stated that

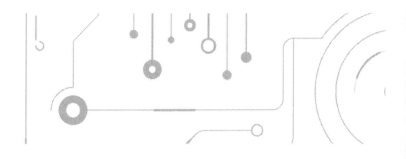

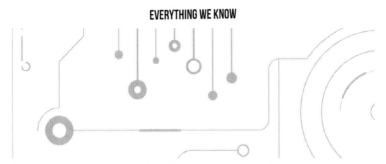

he was hoping to get the chance to write the musical scores

for the entire new trilogy. Abrams made further statements

on this at a Star Trek Into Darkness conference on April 29,

stating, "Again, for Star Wars, it's very early days, but I believe

that, going forward, John Williams will be doing that film

because he was there long before I was." On July 27, 2013,

a video of Williams confirming he would score the new film

was screened at Star Wars Celebration Europe II.

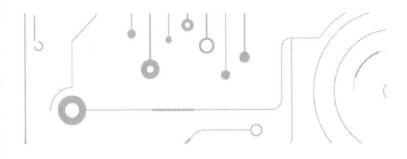

In May 2013, it was revealed that production of Episode VII would take place in the United Kingdom. All of the six other movies of the Star Wars franchise had been partly produced in the U.K., notably in the Elstree, Shepperton, Leavesden, Ealing and Pinewood Studios. Michael Kaplan, who designed the costumes for Abrams' Star Trek films has also signed on to costume Episode VII.

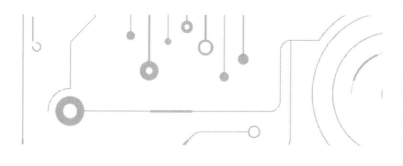

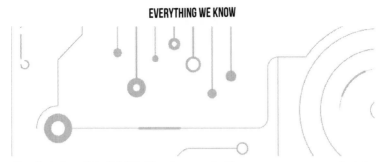

On October 24, 2013, Kasdan and Abrams were revealed to have been rewriting Arndt's script. On November 7, 2013, Lucasfilm announced that the film would be released on December 18, 2015. On November 9, 2013, it was announced that the Fox fanfare will not be in the opening of Star Wars Episode VII. On November 19, 2013, StarWars.com confirmed that R2-D2 will appear in the film. The droid was provided and overseen by members of the R2-D2 Builders Club.

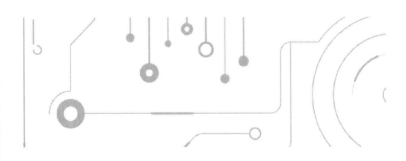

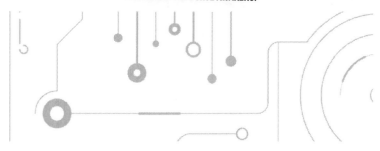

Disney Studios chairman Alan Horn revealed on December 13, 2013, that the estimated budget for Star Wars Episode VII would be at least $200 million. At a Television Critics Association press tour on January 19, 2014, Abrams announced that the script for Episode VII had been finished and that the movie was going "full steam ahead" and in "deep pre-production."

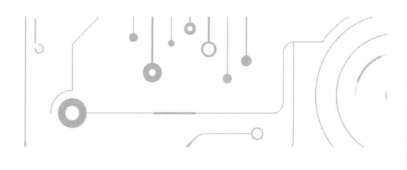

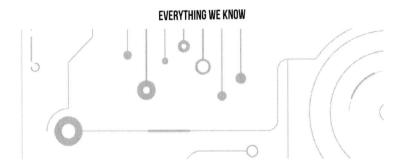

On January 20, 2015, George Lucas revealed in an interview with Cinema Blend that Disney had opted not to use his story treatment for Episode VII and made up their own story instead.

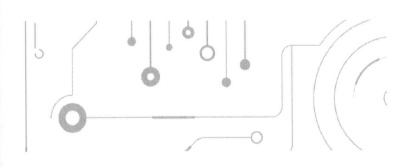

"Part of the experience of [Star Wars] in my life was coming down from that, putting it behind me. We had a beginning, middle, and an end. And I certainly, in a million years, never expected to return. I thought, even if they do more trilogies, my story is over."
- Mark Hammil

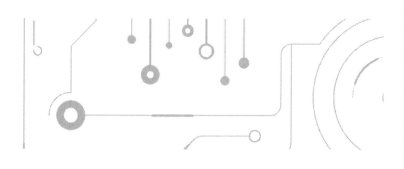

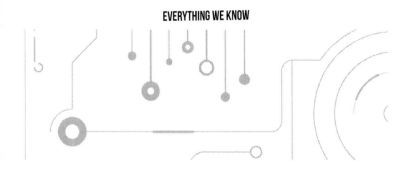

Mark Hamill commented about the sequels in late February 2013 stating that "they are talking to us" and he is scheduled to meet with writer Michael Arndt and Kathleen Kennedy. Hamill stated that so far nobody has signed a contract though there appears to be interest in the entire cast. Hamill went on to say that George Lucas would like to get Peter Mayhew and Anthony Daniels back for the new films as well. Mark Hamill feels that he will return to be "an Obi-Wan type role." In March

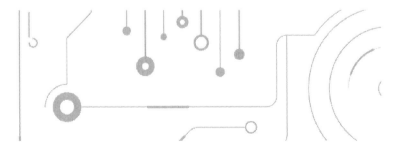

2013, Fisher confirmed she will return as Princess Leia. A day later Lucas confirmed that Hamill, Ford and Fisher were in the final stages of negotiations and that all three were in discussions to return prior to the Disney sale. Lucas then said, "Maybe I'm not supposed to say that. I think they want to announce that with some big whoop-de-do, but we were negotiating with them. I won't say whether the negotiations were successful or not".

On January 20, 2014, Carrie Fisher gave an interview

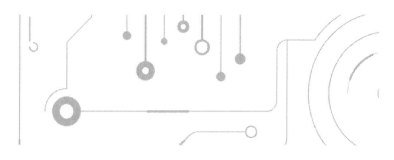

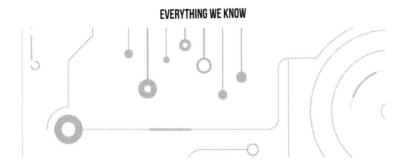

to TV Guide and mentioned that she, Harrison Ford, and Mark

Hamill would all be reporting to work in March or April. This

was verified by Lucasfilm on April 29, 2014.

During an interview promoting the 2014 remake of

RoboCop, actor Gary Oldman confirmed with Sky Movies that

he was indeed approached for a role in the upcoming film. Oth-

er actors such as Ewan McGregor and Billy Dee Williams have

expressed interest in returning, though no official statement has

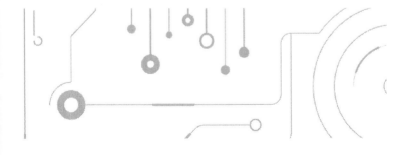

been released regarding their involvement. Alan Horn con-

firmed rumors of talks with Breaking Bad actor Jesse Plemons.

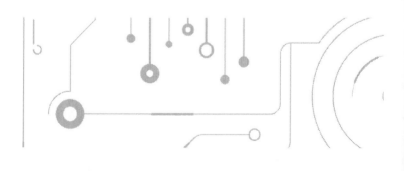

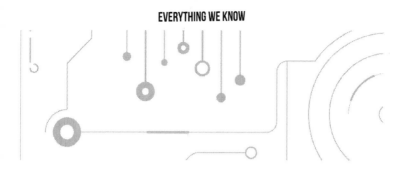

"I've learned to be very careful about Star Wars. If I say, 'There will be no skateboards in Star Wars'... that gets headlines."
- Alan Horn
Disney Chairman

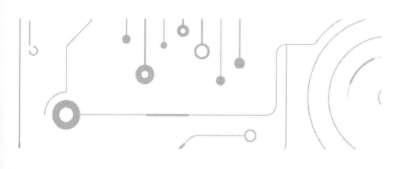

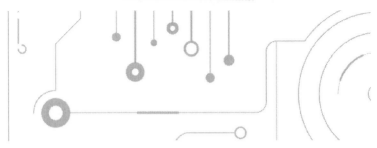

On March 17, 2014, StarWars.com announced that Episode VII would begin principal photography at Pinewood Studios in May 2014, and would be set thirty years after the events of Star Wars: Episode VI Return of the Jedi. They also confirmed that the film will star a trio of young leading actors alongside "some very familiar faces." On April 5, 2014, it was revealed that filming on Star Wars Episode VII had already begun, with second unit work taking place in Iceland and Abu Dhabi.

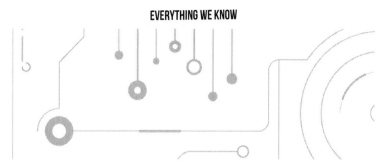

On April 7, 2014, reports surfaced claiming that Peter Mayhew would reprise the role of Chewbacca in Star Wars Episode VII. On April 25, Lucasfilm announced their plans for a new continuity that excluded the existing Expanded Universe, and confirmed that Episode VII and its sequels will not adhere to any existing continuity. This was followed on April 29 by the official release of the cast list for the movie. Mark Hamill, Carrie Fisher, Harrison Ford, Kenny Baker, Peter Mayhew and Anthony Dan-

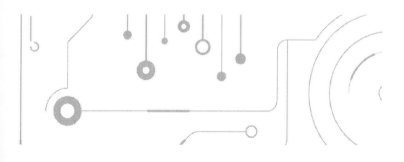

iels would return to reprise their roles as the main characters of

the original trilogy, and they will be joined by a number of new

actors in leading roles: John Boyega, Daisy Ridley, Adam Driver,

Oscar Isaac, Andy Serkis, Domhnall Gleeson, and Max von Sy-

dow. Denis Lawson was asked to reprise his role as Wedge An-

tilles from the original trilogy, but declined, stating that it would

have "bored" him. The production team built a new C-3PO suit

to accommodate Daniels.

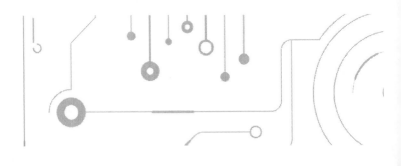

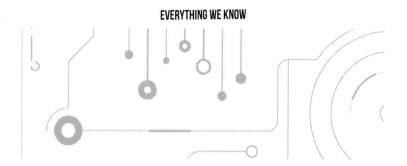

On May 16, 2014, production officially began on the film at

Pinewood Studios. Daniel Mindel—who had previously worked

with Abrams as director of photography—returned to collab-

orate with the director on the film. Reportedly, one sequence

was shot with IMAX cameras. On June 11, the 71-year old

Harrison Ford broke his left leg when a hydraulic door at Pine-

wood Studios fell down and hit him, and was airlifted to John

Radcliffe Hospital in Oxford. His recovery forced him to drop

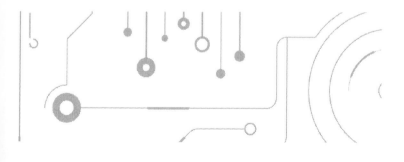

out of filming for eight weeks. On June 28, actor Andy Serkis

confirmed that The Imaginarium Studios will be involved with

performance capture on the film, as well as all future Star Wars

projects. Serkis also confirmed that the character he plays in the

film will utilize performance capture. On July 6, Lucasfilm con-

firmed that actors Crystal Clarke and Pip Andersen were cast in

the film through open casting calls in the United Kingdom. They

also revealed that production would take a two-week hiatus in

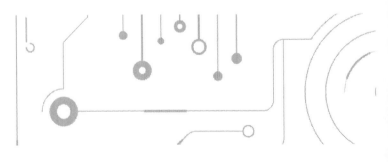

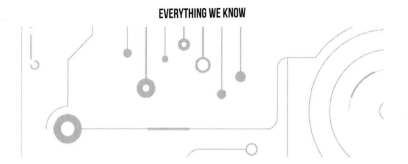

August to accommodate Harrison Ford's leg injury. Afterwards shooting will resume, and conclude later in the fall. Abrams, Hamill, and Daisy Ridley spent three days filming at Skellig Michael in County Kerry, Ireland.

On November 6, 2014, the official Star Wars Twitter account announced that the film had completed principal photography. The post gave the official title for the film as Star Wars: The Force Awakens, and was accompanied by a title card for the

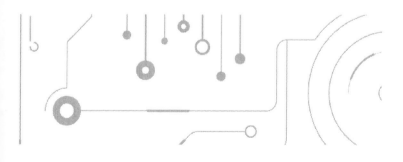

new name that, like the original trilogy, excluded the "Episode"

subtitle.

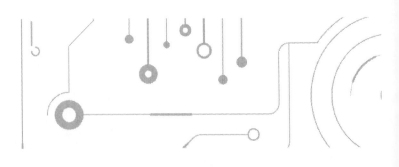

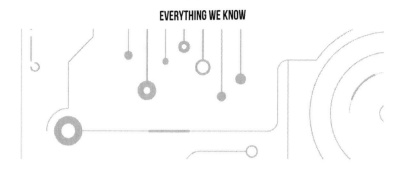

"We're living in such a different age now. It's like a competition to see who can leak information faster than the next guy. I don't get it. I'm keeping my fingers crossed that they don't get a copy of the script and leak the whole thing on the Internet."
- Mark Hammil

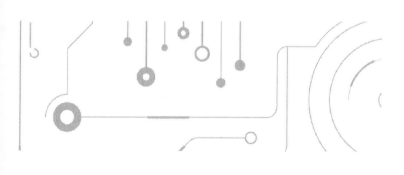

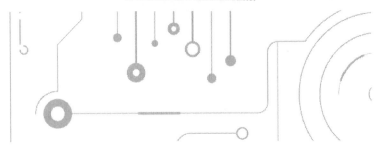

Following Disney's acquisition of Lucasfilm in 2012, its "imag-ineers" began developing Star Wars-themed expansions to the various Disney theme parks. However, Bob Iger halted work on these expansions until The Force Awakens and other future Star Wars films had reached a point in their development so that elements from those projects could be included.

On May 21, 2014, Disney, Lucasfilm and Bad Robot announced "Force for Change", a charity campaign "dedicated to

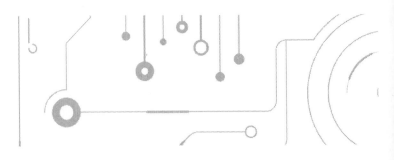

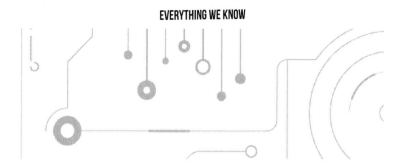

finding creative solutions to some of the world's biggest problems"; Initially, the campaign was focused on contributing to UNICEF. Each person who donated was entered to win a set visit to and appearance in Episode VII. On August 11, Denver, Colorado resident D.C. Barns was announced as the contest's winner. JJ Abrams later released a YouTube video in which he announced that the contest had raised $4.26 million. In August 2014, several of the film's cast and crew participated in the "Ice

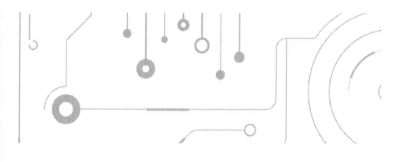

Bucket Challenge", an internet phenomenon whereby one pours water onto one's head as a pledge to donate to the ALS association.

Abrams made a cameo on Last Week Tonight with John Oliver, in which he is seen directing R2-D2 on the set of The Force Awakens. When a fish from Oliver's salmon cannon falls on the script that he's holding, Abrams gets frustrated and quits the film. An 88 second teaser trailer premiered in 30 theaters across

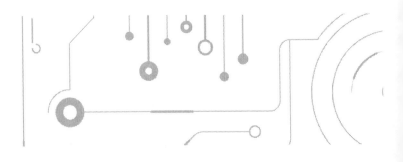

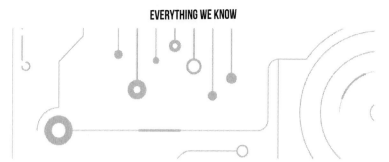

North America and was released online on November 28, 2014.

The trailer was announced via the Bad Robot Productions Twitter account, with a note from Abrams saying fans will see a "tiny peek at what we're working on." The teaser was shown in theaters around the world beginning in December 2014. Character names were revelaed shortly thereafter in online mock collector cards.

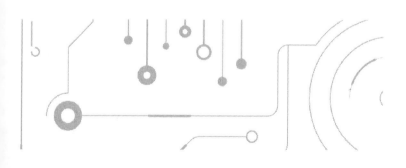

"We are so excited to finally share the cast of Star Wars: Episode VII. It is both thrilling and surreal to watch the beloved original cast and these brilliant new performers come together to bring this world to life, once again. We start shooting in a couple of weeks, and everyone is doing their best to make the fans proud."

- JJ Abrams

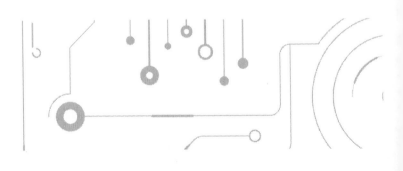

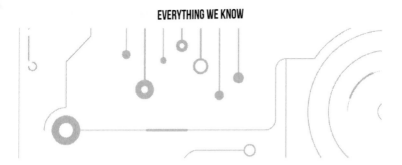

The Force Awakens teaser trailer was released on November 28,

2014, and was screened before every film shown in 30 theaters

across the United States and Canada until November 30. The

trailer was released on YouTube the same day, generating a

record 58.2 million views in its first week, surpassing trailers for

Avengers: Age of Ultron (50.6 million views) and Jurassic World

(53.9 million). It was shown globally in theaters in December

2014.

On December 11, 2014 Abrams and Kennedy released a series of eight mock Topps trading cards revealing the names of several characters. On December 12, 2014 Mark Hamill revealed in an interview to Yahoo Movies that a new droid character called "BB-8" that appeared in the first teaser trailer for the film is not made with any CGI at all, but is rather a working remote-controlled set prop.

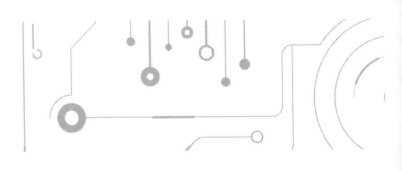

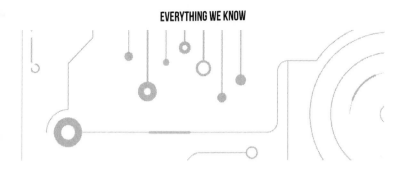

Cinematographer Daniel Mindel stated that The Force Awakens

will use real locations and scale models over computer-gener-

ated imagery to make it aesthetically similar to the original Star

Wars trilogy. Rian Johnson, director of Episode VIII, reiterated

that Abrams will use little CGI and more practical, traditional

special effects, saying: "I think people are coming back around

to [practical effects]. It feels like there is sort of that gravity

pulling us back toward it. I think that more and more people are

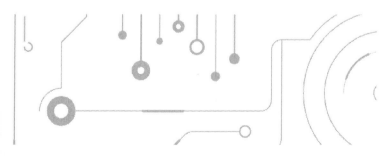

hitting kind of a critical mass in terms of the CG-driven action scene lending itself to a very specific type of action scene, where physics go out the window and it becomes so big so quick."

In February 2014, Industrial Light & Magic (ILM) announced plans to open a facility in London, citing Disney's Star Wars films as a catalyst for the expansion. ILM's Vancouver branch will also work on the special effects for the film.

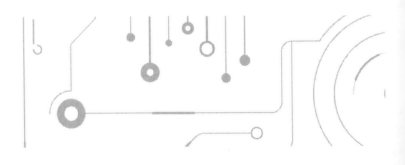

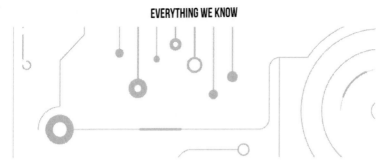

Star Wars: The Force Awakens (also known as Star Wars Episode VII: The Force Awakens) is an upcoming American epic space opera film directed by J. J. Abrams. The seventh installment in the Star Wars film series (excluding spin-offs), it stars John Boyega, Daisy Ridley, Adam Driver, Oscar Isaac, Andy Serkis, Domhnall Gleeson, and Max von Sydow, with Harrison Ford, Carrie Fisher, Mark Hamill, Anthony Daniels, Peter Mayhew and Kenny Baker reprising roles from previous films. The story

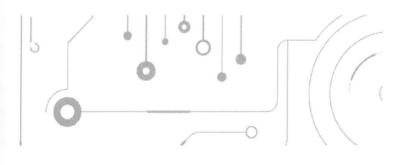

is set approximately 30 years after the events of Return of the

Jedi (1983).

The Force Awakens will be the first film in the planned third

Star Wars trilogy announced after The Walt Disney Company's

acquisition of Lucasfilm in October 2012. It is produced by

Abrams, his long-time collaborator Bryan Burk, and Lucasfilm

president Kathleen Kennedy. Abrams directed the film from a

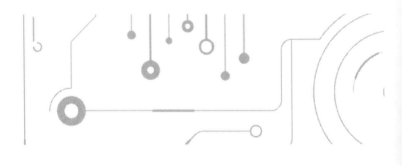

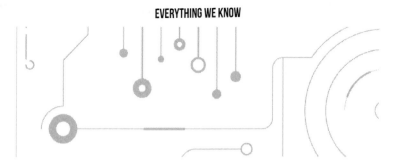

screenplay he co-wrote with Lawrence Kasdan, co-writer of the

original trilogy films The Empire Strikes Back and Return of the

Jedi. Abrams and Kasdan rewrote an initial script by Michael

Arndt, who also wrote the story treatment. John Williams re-

turns to compose the score, and Star Wars creator George Lucas

serves as creative consultant.

The Force Awakens is produced by Walt Disney Pictures, Lucas-

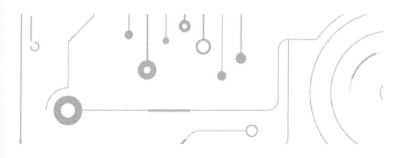

film and Abrams' Bad Robot Productions, and will be distribut-

ed by Walt Disney Studios Motion Pictures. Second-unit filming

began in April 2014 in Abu Dhabi and Iceland, with principal

photography taking place between May and November 2014

in Abu Dhabi, Ireland and Pinewood Studios in England. The

Force Awakens is scheduled for release on December 18, 2015.

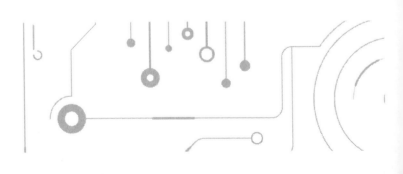

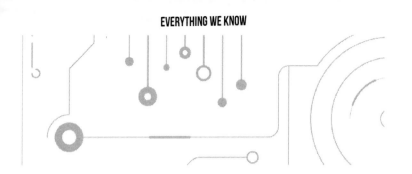

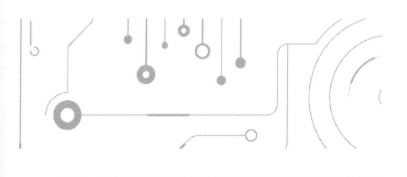

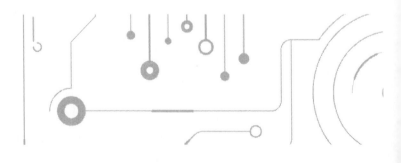

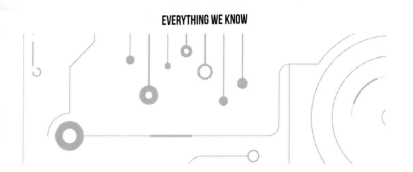

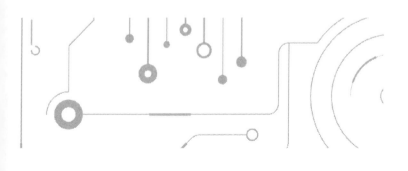

Printed in Great Britain
by Amazon.co.uk, Ltd.,
Marston Gate.

ISBN 9780692390696

90000

We're living in *wild* times.

It should come as no surprise, then, that a book of writing prompts has gone absolutely wild, too. Usually reserved for lonely authors yearning to learn the craft, writing prompts are handy, bite-size directionals designed to point writers of all shapes and sizes down the right path, stimulate their hidden creativity, and leave them leaking creative juices from every hole and pore.

But *Writing Prompts Gone Wild* isn't your average writing prompts book—nor is it for your average scribes: it's for you, the weird, wicked, and wired writers who wish to subvert—and pervert—the norm. So, take this wellspring of sick, uncensored content and get started on your descent to hell, the place most writers end up anyway.

Aaron Barry has been kicked out of more universities than he has fingers to count on. Despite this, they let him teach young, impressionable kids high school English. He's an A-cup angel, can't stand pickles, and frequently dreams in Guns N' Roses lyrics. Vancouver, Canada, is not proud to call him one of their own.

Visit promptsgonewild.com
#promptsgonewild

Humour/Gift
$10.99 U.S.
$13.99 CAN

ISBN 978-1-7771927-0-9

51099

9 781777 192709